For you... because we're friends

Friendship Is A Very Special Thing

The C. R. Gibson Company, Norwalk, Connecticut

You can't buy it or sell it
You can't see it or hear it or touch it
To have it you have to give it away.
Everybody needs it.
It's just about the best thing in the whole world.
What is it?

Friendship!

It's a long word but it isn't nearly long enough to explain all the things that friendship is. Once you have a friend, you start to find out just how many good things are rolled into that one word —

Friendship.

Friendship is a happy thing.
Everybody's always looking for happiness. Well,
friends find it every time they get together —
regardless of the weather.

It's like finding the pot of gold
at the BEGINNING of the rainbow!

Friends don't ever have to make a big fuss or go to a lot of trouble when they're together because friendship is an easy-going thing.

Friends can spend hours together just sitting around, dreaming, not doing much of anything.

That's why it's so much fun to spend a lazy
day with a friend.

Friendship is... a dependable thing.
You can always count on a friend to run an errand
for you or give you a hand — anytime.

Good friends and good talk go together like bacon and eggs, like bees and honey.

Friends have so much to talk about that there never seems to be enough time to say everything they want to say.

Friendship is a funny thing.

It is laughing out loud
and holding your sides
and slapping your knees
and laughing some more.

Sometimes friends are really silly.
They get together and act crazy and
   do nutty stuff and get the giggles.

People say —
"Look at those two.
Did you ever see such a silly pair!"

But friends don't care what people say.
When they feel like being silly, then
silly they will be.

Then ...

There are other times when friendship
is very serious.
Not sad serious.
More of a glad kind of serious.

It may be when friends share a special moment. They may be very quiet because they really don't need any words. And, without saying a thing, each will know how grateful the other is for friendship.

Friendship means never having to say you're bored... because you're not!
Everything friends do together is interesting. Things that might be kind of dull with anyone else (like work!) are fun with a friend.

And if you feel like something
more invigorating, you
can set out on an adventure!

Friendship is an exciting thing!

That's because you never know what's going to happen next when friends get together.

But later on you'll look back on it all
    and think —
"I remember when we did such and such.
Now THAT was a real adventure!"

Friends are alike in so many ways — but not in all ways. That's alright because friendship is an accepting thing.

Friendship is being close in heart
even when you're far apart

It's that missing-you feeling that makes you sit
down and write those words — "Been thinking
of you. Sure wish you were here."

Friendship is a growing thing.
It keeps on getting bigger and stronger the
longer you share it.

And as friendship grows, friends grow, too.
They help each other see new sights and reach
new heights.

Even if you're small, friendship can make
you feel 10 feet tall.

As good as it is,
friendship isn't a perfect thing.
If it was,
most of us would have a hard
time living up to it.

So, once in a great while,
friendship is ...
                    an argument!

But friends can't stay mad at each other
    for long.
That's no fun at all.
For friendship is a forgiving thing.
Soon everything's back the way it used to be.

Even better!

Friendship cheers you up and spurs you on just when you need it the most. And it always makes you try a little harder when you know that your friend is there rooting for you.

Friendship is a sharing thing.
That word "share" is really the most
important part of being friends.

Friends want to share everything — good times, bad times, sad times, glad times, all kinds of times — together.

Friendship — it's about the
best thing in the world.
But no one person can ever possess it.
Friendship takes two —
     a winning combination —
          a dynamic duo —
               a rare pair —
like me and you!

Written by Dean Walley
Illustrated by Bonnie Rutherford
Calligraphy by Maurianna Nolan
Designed by Mansfield Drowne